D0844805

DRUGS **the facts about**

RITALIN

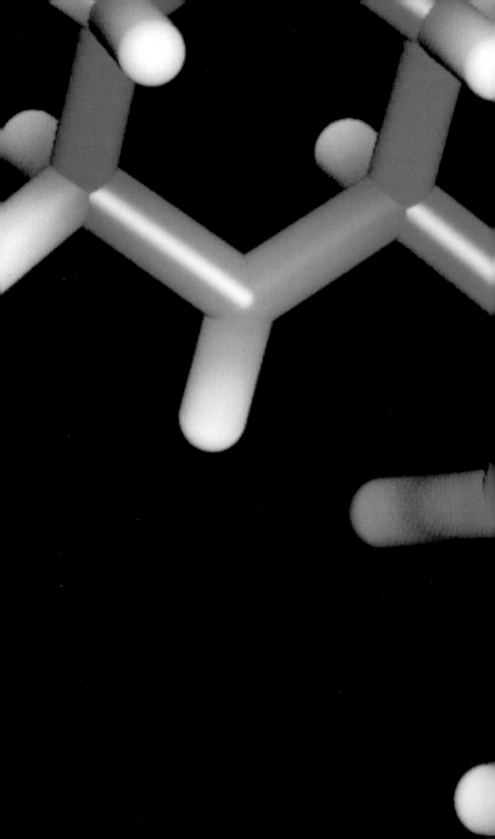

DRUGS **the facts about**
RITALIN

FRANCHA ROFFÉ MENHARD

Marshall Cavendish
Benchmark
New York

For Steven and Jennifer, who taught me everything I know about teens.

Marshall Cavendish Corporation
99 White Plains Road
Tarrytown, NY 10591
www.marshallcavendish.us

Library of Congress Cataloging-in-Publication Data
Menhard, Francha Roffé.

The facts about ritalin / by Francha Roffé Menhard.
p. cm. — (Drugs)
Includes bibliographical references and index.
ISBN-13: 978-0-7614-2245-7
ISBN-10: 0-7614-2245-5
1. Methylphenidate hydrochloride. 2. Attention-deficit hyperactivity disorder—Chemotherapy. 3. Teenagers—Drug use. 4. Children—Drug use. I. Title. II. Series: Drugs (Benchmark Books (Firm)

RJ506.H9M46 2006
618.92'8589061—dc22

Photo research by Joan Meisel

Cover photo: Phototake Inc./Alamy

Alamy: 1, 2–3, 5, Phototake Inc.; 6, Jenny Matthews; 9, VStock; 64, Purestock; Corbis: 34, LWA-Dann Tardif; 41, Wally McNamee; 61, Walter Lockwood; 72, Rune Hellestad; 87, Danny Lehman; Courtesy Landmark College: 49; Peter Arnold, Inc.: 23, Manfred Kage; Photo Researchers, Inc.: 30, Gregory G. Dimijian, MD.; 58, Asa Thorensen; 77, Jim Varney.

Printed in: China
1 3 5 6 4 2

CONTENTS

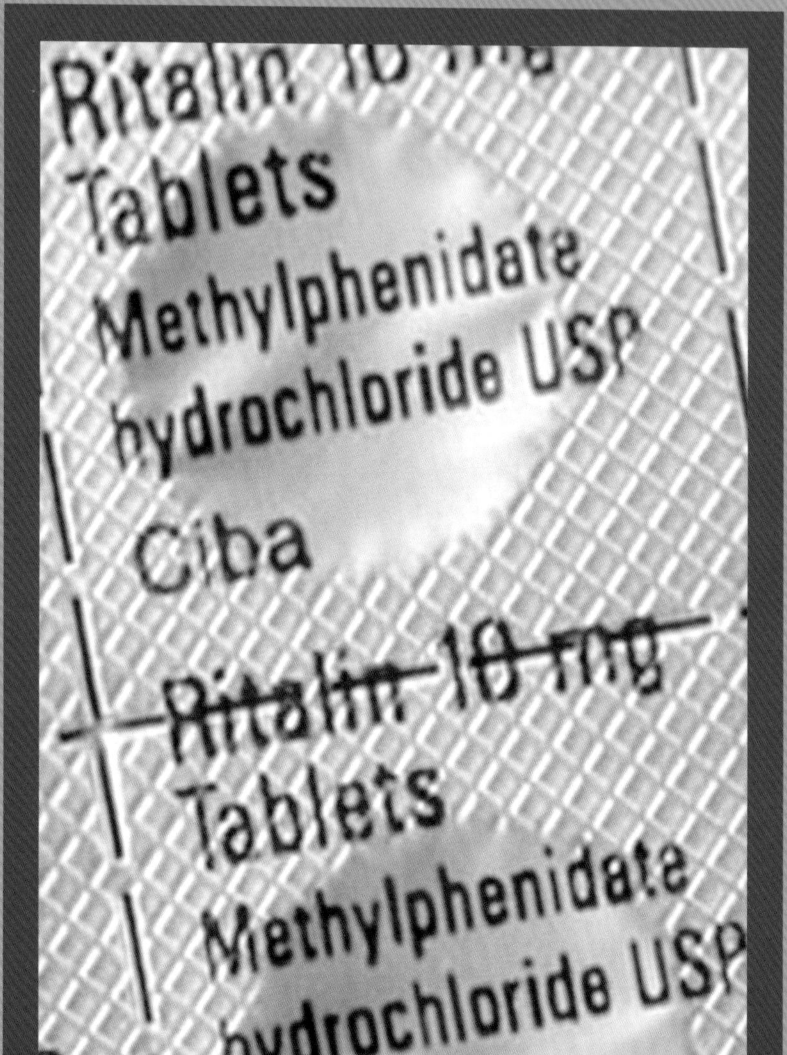
Ritalin
Tablets
Methylphenidate
hydrochloride USP
Ciba
Ritalin 10 mg
Tablets
Methylphenidate
hydrochloride USP
Ciba

1 Ritalin and ADHD

Ritalin is a drug with two faces. It is the drug doctors prescribe for little kids who cannot sit still at school. It is a mild drug, a drug safe enough for five-year-olds to take. For some kids, Ritalin works miracles. For others, it causes unpleasant, though rarely serious, side effects.

The other face of Ritalin is the face of abuse. Ritalin is a chemical cousin of methamphetamine. It is as addictive as cocaine. Both methamphetamine and cocaine are illegal street drugs. The high that Ritalin produces has caused it to become an easily acquired drug of abuse.

Noelle had ADHD, attention deficit hyperactivity disorder. She knew something was wrong with her, but did not know what. She had never done well in school. Her grades were all Cs, Ds, and Fs. She got into fights and was suspended. An avid gymnast, Noelle also had problems during practice. She got distracted and could not concentrate on the balance beam. She tried therapy, and her teachers and coach tried to help her, but that did not help her situation. Noelle grew more and more discouraged.

Toward the end of the fifth grade, Noelle asked her mother if she could try Ritalin because she suspected she had ADHD. In her first year of middle school, her doctor tested her and agreed that Ritalin might help. For Noelle, the medication made a big difference. Suddenly she could focus on her schoolwork. She could work through the necessary steps to complete assignments. It made a big difference at the gym too. Her performance improved by leaps and bounds. Her gymnastics coach could tell on any given day whether she had taken her medication.

After a year, Noelle stopped taking Ritalin. She felt she was not as social or vibrant on Ritalin as she was when she was off the drug. Also, the mother of one of her friends was an herbalist who was promoting a natural alternative to Ritalin. Noelle decided that Ritalin was not good for her. Her problems returned. Her teachers noticed right away, and within a month, she started taking the pills again.

As she approaches high school graduation, Noelle continues to take medication for her ADHD. She is a healthy, intelligent girl, and she still participates in gymnastics. She is beginning to think about attending college or becoming a sports therapist.

BOYS ARE MORE LIKELY THAN GIRLS TO BE DIAGNOSED WITH ADHD. IF A PERSON CAN'T CONCENTRATE, IT CAN BE REALLY HARD TO DO HOMEWORK.

How It Feels to Have ADHD

David Cole hated the way Ritalin made him feel. He described some of those feelings in the book, *Learning Outside The Lines*. David was smarter than most of his peers with ADHD. His IQ was so high that he skipped a grade. But school was completely frustrating for him. By second grade David was spending more time in the hall than in class. He hated school and he hated himself. "Why do I have to be such a spaz all the time?" he wondered. "I hate being such a spaz all the time." Teachers told him, "Buckle down and study harder," or "Focus!" But that advice didn't really help him because he just couldn't focus.

His parents put him on Ritalin, which, he says, at least kept him out of a group home for children with behavioral disorders. "A kid gets a lousy teacher, throws a chair out of total frustration. That kid goes to a group home."

In high school, David spent most of his time in detention. "All day," he wrote. "Six hours sitting still. Winding up tighter and tighter for six hours. By the end of a day in that room, I had nothing left inside but blind rage. Hate. Six hours under lights that gave you a headache after two. I spent six hours fantasizing how I would torture them if I had the chance."

During his sophomore year, David turned to illegal drugs, dropped out of school, and ran away from home. The first time he got high, he wrote, "it was as if someone cut off a straitjacket I didn't even know I was wearing. I stopped trying to follow the rules."

Eventually David decided that school was not designed for people like him. Neat handwriting? Doing long division on paper? Good spelling? The world that depends on these things doesn't exist anymore, David says. Now "we're in a world that depends on information retrieval, presentation, ability to use a computer, work around a problem and find dynamic ways to interact with a problem." That realization led him to an unexpected place: college, and in 2002, David graduated with honors from Brown, an Ivy League university.

Attention Deficit Disorder

It would be difficult to discuss the use of Ritalin without explaining attention disorders. The terms attention deficit disorder (ADD) and attention deficit disorder with hyperactivity (ADHD) describe a condition in which children demonstrate developmentally inappropriate levels of attention, concentration, activity, distractability, and impulsivity. Attention disorders generally begin early in childhood and often continue into the teen years and adulthood. They are probably hereditary and run in families. Experts estimate that between 3 percent and 7.5 percent of all children suffer from attention disorders—some six million in the United States, according to the National Institute of Mental Health. Boys are more likely to be diagnosed than girls. Typically, ADHD in girls is discovered late—or never. Some have called attention disorders in girls the invisible disorder, since their behavior does not attract attention as often as does that of boys. As more research is done, the number of girls being diagnosed is growing.

In ADHD, brain areas regulating attention and inhibition do not work very well. Most children with ADHD are inattentive and impulsive. Boys tend to be hyperactive as well. In teenagers, the hyperactivity often looks like restlessness. For some, paying attention is their biggest problem. This is generally true of girls. Boys with ADHD also have trouble paying attention and are easily distracted, but they are more likely to be hyperactive, impulsive, and disruptive than girls.

Brandon was a child with ADHD who displayed classic symptoms. Even before he started school, he had problems, and by second grade, he was in trouble in school all the time. He forgot to raise his hand and yelled out answers. He often interrupted his teacher when she was speaking to the class and could not stay in his seat. Even though he was smart, he did not finish his work in class. Instead he moved around the room without permission, disturbing the other children. When his teacher or other kids got upset with him, he ran from the classroom. He always found his way to the boiler room in the basement of the school, where the custodian calmed him down, then escorted him back to class.

Brandon's teacher had recognized his behavior as a sign of attention deficit disorder, or what was then called ADD. An attention disorder is a "developmental disorder of self-control," explains Russell Barkley, a leading expert on the subject of attention deficit disorders. It is characterized by problems with attention span, impulse control, and activity level.

The number of people with ADHD is not clear. According to the National Institute of Mental Health, ADHD is one of the most common mental disorders in schoolage children and teens, affecting about 4.1 percent of nine-to seventeen-year-olds. According to Mayo Clinic data from 2001,

Symptoms of ADHD

There are three subtypes of ADHD: predominantly hyperactive-impulsive; inattentive; and combined.

To have ADHD, a person must demonstrate:

- six or more of the symptoms of inattention, or hyperactivity-impulsivity must have been present for at least six months;
- some symptoms that have caused distractability, concentration, and impulse control before seven years of age;
- impairment in at least two settings, such as at school and home;
- clinically significant impairment in social, academic, or occupational functioning.

The symptoms must not occur exclusively during the course of another disorder or be better accounted for by another disorder.

Symptoms of hyperactivity or impulsivity include:

- fidgeting with hands or feet or squirming in seat;
- running about or climbing in situations in which such behavior is inappropriate;
- blurting out answers before questions have been completed.

Symptoms of inattention include:

- failing to give close attention to details or making careless mistakes in schoolwork or other activities;
- difficulty organizing tasks and activities;
- being easily distracted by extraneous stimuli.

Source: *Diagnostic and Statistic Manual of Mental Disorders IV* of the American Psychiatric Association.

7.5 percent have ADHD. The Centers for Disease Control and Prevention estimates that some 1.6 million children between the ages of six and eleven have ADHD (about 7 percent) and about a million of these children take prescription drugs for the condition, though some take drugs other than Ritalin. Boys are about three times as likely to have ADHD as girls. So many children were diagnosed with ADHD and took Ritalin and similar drugs during the 1990s that some people began calling them the ADHD, or Ritalin, generation.

Brandon is a member of the Ritalin generation. A psychiatrist diagnosed him with a classic case of attention deficit disorder and hyperactivity, today called ADHD, and prescribed Ritalin, the most popular brand of methylphenidate.

Ritalin is a stimulant that reduces restlessness and hyperactivity in people with attention disorders and hyperactivity. Doctors most commonly prescribe it for schoolage children but also for preschoolers and adults. Ritalin helps with attention, organization, impulse control, and fine motor skills. It also helps children complete tasks more quickly. Because Ritalin helps children focus, they are better able to control impulsive behavior.

For many people with ADHD, Ritalin serves a function similar to corrective lenses for children with vision problems. It is a tool that helps them deal with their disability. It helps them to calm down and to concentrate.

On Ritalin, Brandon could stay still in class. He could do his schoolwork. He didn't get into trouble all the time. And when he visited the custodian, it was because he wanted to—not because he was running away from his classroom.

ADHD Symptoms

Throughout elementary school, Brandon's mother followed his progress closely. She made sure the school nurse gave him his medications throughout the school day. She chose teachers who understood his condition. They set limits for Brandon and helped him learn to set limits for himself. They broke down assignments into manageable chunks and taught him to manage homework this way. "Everybody in the school knew that Brandon had ADD," his mother said. "When he got squirrelly, his friends would remind him to take his medicine. Even the principal—not known to make allowances for anyone—made allowances for him."

But other kids made fun of him because of his disorder. They learned how to push Brandon until he lashed out at them, then laughed at him when he got into trouble. He felt stigmatized by his disorder. He hated having everyone in elementary school know about it. When he went to middle school, he started using his middle name, James, leaving behind the association of Brandon with ADD. Today his family and his oldest friends still call him Brandon, but everyone he met after elementary school knows him as James.

Brandon did not like the way Ritalin made him feel. "It was like it created a kind of disconnect," he said struggling to describe the feeling, "between me—and *me*." Still, he continued taking Ritalin until age fifteen, when his psychiatrist told him that he was old enough to decide for himself if he wanted to take the medication or not. Today there are many ADHD drugs to choose from, and Brandon may have found one that suits him better. Still treatment with stimulant medications does not work for everyone, and unpleasant side effects mean that the dropout rate in stimulant treatment is high, reports the January 2005 *Harvard Mental Health Letter.*

Once Brandon stopped taking Ritalin, his life went into a downward spiral. Middle school had been difficult. High school became a nightmare, with the exception of a welding class he attended each afternoon at a special vocational school. He hated what he saw as the pointless busywork of the classroom and could not force himself to do it. His grades dropped. He got into trouble with teachers and other students. He experimented with drugs, starting with marijuana and methamphetamine, a chemical cousin of Ritalin. He was self-medicating, his mother said. He was so unhappy that his parents pulled him out in his senior year. He took and passed the GED, an exam students take to earn a certificate that is the equivalent of a high school diploma. He passed easily.

Brandon was not alone. Twenty-five percent to 37 percent of students with ADHD do not graduate from high school—versus one percent of students without ADHD, though half of those who do not graduate will get a General Education Diploma by taking the GED test.

Adults with ADHD
About 4 percent of all adults in the United States—more than 8 million adults—are affected, with men and women affected in equal numbers. Adults with ADHD are more likely than other people to have trouble in their lives. Many drift into delinquency, abuse other drugs, and move from low-level job to low-level job, as did Brandon. They have more serious car accidents, and a hard time managing money and handling day-to-day responsibilities. Teen girls with ADHD are more likely to get pregnant.

With school behind him, Brandon struggled to fit into the adult world and the work force. As with many adults, his ADHD continued to cause problems. Though he worked hard and was smart, he was still impulsive and this often got him into trouble with his bosses. Sometimes they fired him. Sometimes he quit. He lived at home and continued to abuse drugs. Attending college was not an option at the time. For students with ADHD who choose to go on to college, the odds are against graduating. Only 5 percent of students with ADHD will complete a college program, compared to 35 percent of the population without the disorder.

What turned Brandon around was getting caught with illegal drugs. At twenty-four, he found himself in drug court for possession of methamphetamines. After time in a rehabilitation program and the threat of going to jail hanging over his head, Brandon has pulled together all the strategies he has learned for managing his ADHD. He has his first real job, working in the outdoors, setting up cellular phone towers. Only time will tell if he will be successful, but his mother is hopeful. "He likes the feeling of success, and he likes living on his own."

Many adults only find out that they have ADHD when their children start having trouble in school. That is what happened with both of Brandon's parents. Nonetheless, both his parents have successful careers. They both work in professions that do not require extensive paperwork and let them move around freely. His mother owns a hair salon, and his father is a chef. His mother hopes that the example of his parents' stability and success despite their ADHD will help Brandon find his own road to success and fulfillment.

Ritalin and Other Forms of Methylphenidate

The U.S. Food and Drug Administration (FDA) is the nation's official consumer protection and health agency. Its team of approximately nine thousand public health employees includes physicians, nurses, consumer safety officers, lawyers, and scientists, with specialties ranging from biomaterials engineering to pharmacology. The agency's main job is to ensure that the food and drugs Americans consume are safe, effective, and truthfully labeled.

The FDA has approved several stimulant medicines for treating ADHD: dextroamphetamine, Dexedrine and generics; methamphetamine, Desoxyn; an amphetamine-dextroamphetamine combination, Adderall; and methylphenidate, Ritalin, and generics. Methylphenidate is the most commonly used of these drugs.

Ritalin was also the most popular form of methylphenidate for some forty years and remains the most well-known trade name for the prescription drug. Most people still think Ritalin when they think of medication for attention deficit disorders, no matter what drug is actually prescribed. For these reasons, this book generally uses Ritalin to refer to all forms of methylphenidate.

Methylphenidate (methyl a-phenyl-2 piperidineacetate hydrochloride — $C_{14}H_{19}NO_2$) is not an amphetamine but a chemical cousin of amphetamine that works in much the same way. It is a white, odorless, fine crystalline powder. It comes in 5, 10, and 20 mg tablets. The tablets are usually white or yellow. Sustained release Ritalin comes in 20 mg tablets. Inactive ingredients—the ingredients that have no methylphenidate in them—may include dye, lactose, magnesium stearate, polyethylene glycol, starch, sucrose, talc, and tragacanth. One dose of Ritalin lasts up to six hours. One dose of long-acting or sustained release Ritalin lasts six to eight hours. Taken as prescribed, Ritalin is an effective medicine for about 80 percent of children with attention deficit disorders. In 2006, the FDA approved the first skin patch for children with ADHD. Each patch delivers 10, 15, 20, or 30 mg of methylphenidate and lasts nine hours.

How Ritalin Works
No one knows exactly how Ritalin works in the brain, but researchers continue to study the process.

After someone takes Ritalin, the active ingredient, methylphenidate, enters the bloodstream, which carries it quickly to the brain. The brain is made up of billions of nerve cells (neurons). Most neurons have three important parts:

- the cell body, which contains the nucleus and directs the activities of the neuron;
- dendrites, short fibers that receive messages from other neurons and relay them to the cell body;
- an axon, one long single fiber that carries messages from the cell body to dendrites of other neurons.

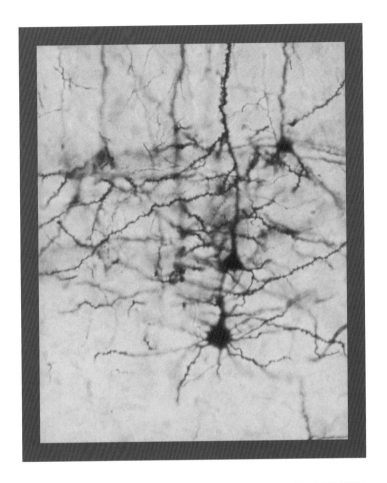

DENDRITES ARE SHORT FIBERS THAT ACT AS RECEPTORS OF INFORMATION FROM ONE NEURON TO ANOTHER.

The neuron sends a message to another neuron by releasing a neurotransmitter from its axon into the small space that separates the two neurons. This space is called a synapse. The neurotransmitter crosses the synapse and attaches to specific places on the dendrites of the neighboring neuron. These places are called receptors. Once the neurotransmitter has relayed its message, it is either used up or taken back up into the first neuron, where it is recycled for future use.

In the past, scientists believed that Ritalin affected the structures in the brain that contain a chemical called dopamine. Dopamine is sometimes called the pleasure neurotransmitter because it makes people feel good. When something good happens, certain axons release dopamine. The dopamine attaches to receptors on dendrites of neighboring neurons to transmit the pleasure message. The process stops when the receptors release the dopamine back to the neuron that released it. That neuron stores the dopamine until it is needed again.

Researchers thought that Ritalin short-circuited the process of storing dopamine for recycling (or reuptake). Reuptake occurs when the neuron takes back the whole neurotransmitter molecule. Once the neurons take the dopamine neurotransmitters back from the synapse, they can no longer bind to the pleasure receptors. Like amphetamine, its chemical cousin Ritalin interferes with this process. It fools the neurons, and they take up the drug as if it were actually dopamine. Once it gets inside a neuron, Ritalin tells the neuron to release dopamine.

However, recent laboratory tests suggest that what Ritalin does may be more complex. It may interact with a different neurotransmitter, serotonin, as well as with dopamine. Ritalin may regulate the balance between levels of serotonin and dopamine and calm the hyperactivity, restlessness, and inattention of ADHD. The brain has at least fifteen different receptors that bind to serotonin, so the next step is for researchers to find out which of those receptors Ritalin targets. This would allow pharmaceutical companies to design a new medication that would target only those specific receptors. Such a drug would be more precise and have fewer side effects.

Ritalin and the Body
The effects of Ritalin are usually mild when patients take the drug as directed. Patients over age six with ADHD usually begin by taking between 5 and 10 mg from one to three times a day and adjust the dose depending on its effects. For most patients, doctors increase the dose gradually by 5 to 10 mg weekly. For some patients who get worse on Ritalin, doctors may reduce the dosage or discontinue it. The dose should not exceed 60 mg daily, even in adults. Its most common side effects are loss of appetite, insomnia (trouble sleeping), abdominal pain, and headache.

Names for Methylphenidate

Ritalin	Concerta
Methylin	Focalin
Metadate	

Safe Prescriptions

Ritalin is generally safe as long as it is correctly prescribed. Sometimes doctors confuse ADHD with learning disabilities, depression, and anxiety. They may also confuse restlessness with hyperactivity. In such cases, Ritalin is prescribed when other treatment is called for.

Diagnosing ADHD takes good clinical detective work, says child psychiatrist Ismail Sendi of Michigan's Henry Ford Health System. Sendi tested 388 Michigan children who were taking Ritalin. He found that only sixty-seven had been correctly diagnosed. The other 82 percent should have been getting treatment for another disorder.

One reason so many are misdiagnosed, Sendi says, is that busy primary care physicians often have only fifteen or twenty minutes to diagnose the disorder. Sendi sometimes spends five days evaluating patients. Another reason is that a small number of doctors write a large percentage of prescriptions. In Michigan, for example, 5 percent of doctors write 50 percent of prescriptions. In rural Dickinson County in the Upper Peninsula almost 8 percent of the population took Ritalin or generic methylphenidate between 1997 and 1999, the latest date for which such data are available. The national average at that time was one percent.

Source: Michigan Public Radio

Ritalin has other common side effects:

- heightened alertness
- euphoria
- impairment of voluntary movement
- irregular or rapid heartbeat
- nausea and vomiting
- skin rash
- drowsiness

About 20 percent of children stop taking Ritalin in favor of other drugs, such as the amphetamine Adderall or an antidepressant. These drugs also have side effects—but people have different reactions to different drugs, so those who switch do so because the side effects of the other medications are easier for them to tolerate.

Abusing Ritalin
In recent years, Ritalin has become one of the most abused prescription drugs. Abuse is using the drug without a prescription, taking more than is prescribed, snorting, or injecting the drug instead of taking it orally as prescribed. People abuse Ritalin for a high similar to that of amphetamines and cocaine. Cocaine is shorter-acting and has more of a punch, but in general, the human body cannot tell the difference between cocaine, amphetamines, and Ritalin.

Between 1988 and 1998, the number of students diagnosed with ADHD increased 280 percent.

Between 25 percent and 50 percent of children with ADHD will be held back a grade at least once, according to Russell Barkley, professor of psychiatry and neurology and author of numerous books on ADHD. Three percent of adults with ADHD will attend graduate school or complete a graduate degree, compared to 16 percent of adults without ADHD.

People with ADHD Can Help Themselves
Ritalin and other medications do not cure attention disorders. They control the disorder, much as insulin controls diabetes but does not cure it. And the medication alone cannot control attention deficit disorder. Children with ADHD must also take steps to help control their disorder, just as children with diabetes have to test their blood and eat foods that help to keep their disease in check. They must make the most of their strengths and work to overcome their weaknesses. They must cooperate with the medication.

Some students with ADHD use their disorder as an excuse not to try, but many students like Noelle have found their own ways to cope with the disorder. They choose not to make ADHD their whole identity. As Dr. Patricia Quinn says, "The disorder is part of who you are and, yes, you have to control it. But it doesn't define you. It's okay to have attention disorder, so long as you know what to do about it." They learn as much as they can about ADHD and the strategies that can help them help themselves. If they have questions, they ask their doctor or a school nurse. They set realistic goals and try to be honest about their strengths and weaknesses. They know their rights.

They ask for more time on tests if they need it or a front seat away from distractions. Some have started support groups with other classmates who have ADHD. They are careful with their medications. They report side effects to their parents or doctor. They figure out a way to take medicine on time. Some set an alarm or use an appointment to remind them. And they never, never share their medicine.

THE SYNTHESIZING OF EPHEDRA, A PLANT WHICH GROWS IN THE CHIHUAHUAN DESERT IN THE SOUTHWESTERN REGION OF THE UNITED STATES, WAS THE FIRST STEP IN THE DIRECTION OF FINDING MEDICINE THAT COULD HELP CHILDREN WHO HAD DIFFICULTY WITH HYPERACTIVITY.

2 HISTORY OF RITALIN USE AND ABUSE

The history of Ritalin is intertwined with that of attention deficit disorders as well as with the history of amphetamines. In 1887, L. Edeleano first synthesized amphetamine in a laboratory in Germany. He called it phenylisopropylamine. In 1919, Japanese chemist A. Ogata synthesized methamphetamine, stronger and easier to make than amphetamine. In the 1920s, militaries throughout the world began to prescribe amphetamine for soldiers on the battlefield. Around the same time, researchers tested amphetamines in humans, and it proved useful for people with asthma and other respiratory problems.

ADHD is a not a new disease, although the name is somewhat recent. In 1902, Dr. George Still identified a new condition for the Royal College of

Physicians of London. He noticed in children a "defect in moral control" and a lack of ability to "control their activity for the good of others and the good of themselves." Still described two children. The five-year-old girl, he reported, was "extremely passionate," and "if crossed in any way she will throw herself down on the floor and scream and kick." This "wantonly mischievous girl" turned on the water taps and left them running. She would not obey, and spanking her had "little or no restraining effect." The eleven-year-old boy was "extremely excitable and very passionate." With little provocation, this boy went up to children he hardly knew and grabbed their toys—not because he wanted the toys himself, "but apparently because he enjoys their grief."

In 1927, Gordon Alles, a graduate student at the University of California Los Angeles, synthesized ephedrine, an extract from the ephedra plant used to treat asthma. He failed to synthesize the drug he wanted, but during his experiments, he tried some of the drug he made instead. Suddenly he was more alert and less tired. Alles patented this drug and in 1932 sold it to the pharmaceutical company Smith Kline & French. They marketed it as Benzedrine, a derivative of the stimulant amphetamine, for the treatment of asthma and nasal congestion.

Charles Bradley was a pediatrician who had studied neurology in Philadelphia when he came to the Emma Pendleton Bradley Home in East

Providence, Rhode Island. There, he carried out brain studies of the children. Some of the tests caused the children to have terrible headaches, so he tried Benzedrine to ease their pain.

The drug did not cure the children's headaches, but it did make school easier for them. The children at the home called the medication "arithmetic pills" because they seemed to be able to sit still and concentrate on their studies. Suddenly, they grew interested in what their class was studying. They wanted to finish as much schoolwork as they could. They could understand better and do more accurate work.

After that, Bradley expanded the use of these amphetamines to other children with behavior problems. He reported the results of his studies in 1937, but his article did not get much attention, even though it pointed out the strange paradox that stimulants that keyed up adults somehow calmed children down.

A Whirlwind of Frenzied Activity

The effect of Benzedrine in children remained just an article in a medical journal for more than ten years, but the study of children's behavior problems was moving ahead. In the 1940s and 1950s, more and more people agreed that the extremely active behavior of many children—especially boys— interfered with their daily activities. And things were worse at school. They could not sit still or plan ahead or finish their assignments. Researchers and

Students with ADHD often find school frustrating.

other professionals began to search for a name to describe these behavioral problems. Minimal brain damage and minimal brain dysfunction were several of the early names for the disorder which would come to be called ADHD. People began to notice that the number of children with these syndromes seemed to be on the rise.

Meanwhile Leandro Panizzon synthesized methylphenidate (brand name Ritalin) in 1944, and Meier replicated this synthesis in 1954. In about 1955, the Swiss pharmaceutical company Ciba-Geigy marketed the drug to the elderly. The U.S. Food and Drug Administration (FDA) approved methyl-phenidate for treatment of drug-induced lethargy, mild depression, and narcolepsy.

Since methylphenidate was very similar to Dexedrine, which was already being used for children with behavior disorders, it was logical to study methylphenidate for the treatment of these disorders, too.

Methylphenidate—MPH for short—was first synthesized in 1944. In 1950, Ciba Pharmaceutical Company received a patent for the drug and began to test it on humans. The FDA granted approval for the use of the drug in 1955 as a mild stimulant indicated in chronic fatigue and depressive states, particularly those associated with reserpine or chlorpromazine therapy. Ritalin is also helpful in narcolepsy and psychoneuroses and psychoses associated with depression. Nasal congestion sometimes seen with rauwolfia derivatives is frequently alleviated. In certain psychotic or senile patients, Ritalin has been found to improve behavior patterns.

In 1957, Ciba introduced MPH in the United States under the brand name Ritalin. Doctors prescribed it for fatigue, depression, and narcolepsy, a disease that causes people to fall asleep unexpectedly. They also prescribed it in the 1960s for psychosis associated with depression and for people who had overdosed on barbiturates, a depressant drug that causes relaxation and sleepiness. In 1960 Ritonic appeared on the market. This tonic was a cocktail of methylphenidate, hormones, and vitamins. It was advertised to improve mood and boost vitality. In 1963, Ciba marketed it for prescription to children with functional behavior problems. During the 1960s, researchers began to focus on Ritalin as a treatment for hyperactive child syndrome, hyperkinetic reaction, hyperkinetic impulse disorder, and hyperactivity, early names for ADHD.

In the 1960s, researchers began to study methylphenidate in earnest. Five studies in 1963, including the first placebo-controlled study, agreed that methylphenidate was useful in the treatment of ADHD. Pediatric neurologist J. Gordon Millichap compared the effectiveness of Ritalin and amphetamine. After reviewing the literature, he concluded in 1968 that "methylphenidate is the drug of choice" based on a comparison of all reported cases treated with the drug—of 337 patients, 84 percent improved, compared with a 69 percent improvement in the 415 patients treated with amphetamines. His research did not look at dose, patient population, or response measures, however, so it was not really possible to say definitively that Ritalin was better than amphetamines.

His study led many people to believe that Ritalin was, in fact, better than amphetamines, even though two 1963 placebo-controlled studies—studies in which some of the participants take real drugs and others take sugar pills—showed that amphetamine and Ritalin are not all that different. Furthermore, Dr. Russell Barkley's 1977 review of sixteen previous studies found the same. Fifteen studies using amphetamines showed 74 percent improvement, compared to fourteen with methylphenidate that showed 77 percent improvement that is not statistically significant. Still, the belief that Ritalin was better than amphetamines persisted, and researchers carried out more research studies on methylphenidate than on amphetamine during the 1970s and the 1980s. Their research, along with the marketing of Ritalin in pediatric journals, helped to boost the perception of Ritalin as the drug of choice. Additional comparative studies reported similar effectiveness and safety.

Throughout the 1980s and 1990s, prescribing Ritalin for children with ADHD grew more commonplace, and hundreds of thousands of students lined up outside school nurses' offices across the United States for their Ritalin pills every day. Ritalin dominated the market for ADHD drugs until 1996, when the FDA approved the marketing of the amphetamine-based Adderall. In 2002, Novartis received FDA approval for Ritalin LA, a long-acting form of Ritalin that eliminates the need for a midday dose.

History of Ritalin Abuse
Ritalin abuse began quietly in the early 1990s, although some people abused it during the 1960s and 1970s for a quick high or as an easy way to lose weight. During the 1980s, cocaine was the drug of choice among adults, but for teens, Ritalin was easier to acquire. Soon teens were scoring pills from friends, crushing them, and snorting the powder in

the bathroom at school. In 1995, one teen said, "Out of ten people I know, maybe one has seen or tried cocaine, but nine of them have done Ritalin."

Trends in Ritalin Use and Abuse
No one knows exactly how many people legally use Ritalin, but the American Academy of Pediatrics estimates that 4.5 percent of elementary school students, 4.3 percent of middle school students, and 1.3 percent of high school students take Ritalin by prescription. That works out to some 33 million in elementary school and 17 million in high school, according to a 2005 U.S. Census Bureau press release.

Prescription of Ritalin and its chemical cousins varies widely throughout the United States. The drug is much more frequently prescribed for boys, who get 75 percent of Ritalin prescriptions, the San Francisco *Chronicle* reported in 2003. Getting a prescription for Ritalin depends on race and wealth, too.

White, suburban elementary schoolchildren are more than twice as likely to take Ritalin as black students. For example, only 9.5 percent of six-to-fourteen-year-olds enrolled in the North Carolina Medicaid program in 1998 received prescriptions for stimulant medication, including Ritalin. Some 18 percent of white North Carolina males not enrolled in Medicaid programs received prescriptions from their doctors. Similarly, one small 1999 study of students near Richmond, Virginia, found that 17 percent of Caucasian boys took Ritalin and similar drugs for ADHD, compared to 9 percent of African-American boys.

Where children live also plays a role in whether their doctor prescribes Ritalin. Children were most likely to be prescribed brand name and generic Ritalin in New Hampshire, Vermont, and Michigan, the FDA reported in 1999. Children in New Mexico and Hawaii were least likely to be prescribed the drug. In fact, children in just one county in Virginia—Henrico—took more Ritalin than all the children in all the counties in the state of Hawaii. Hawaii has six times as many children as Henrico County.

There has been a sharp increase in prescription Ritalin use since it became popular in the 1980s. The number of children with prescriptions for ADHD, including prescriptions for Ritalin, Adderall, and Strattera—which is not a stimulant—rose 23 percent between 2000 and 2003. ADHD drug prescriptions for pre-schoolers were up 49 percent. Between 1991 and 2001, production of Ritalin and its generic counterparts increased sevenfold. Former Congressman Bob Schaffer (R-Colorado) attributed this increase to Federal incentives.

At a hearing of the Subcommittee on Oversight and Investigations of the Committee on Education and the Workforce, Schaffer said:

In 1990, Supplemental Security Income [. . .] was opened to include low-income parents whose children were labeled with ADHD. . . .

This allowed some families to receive more than $450 per month per child. . . . In 1989, children citing mental impairments including ADHD but not retardation made up only 5 percent of disabled kids on SSI; and that figure rose to nearly 25 percent by 1995.

In 1991, the Department of Education made hundreds of special education dollars available every year for children labeled with ADHD. After that [. . .] schools could receive more than $400 per student under IDEA for each child diagnosed with ADHD and in need of special education.

Shaffer does not mention Section 504 of the Vocational Rehabilitation Act, though he alludes to it. Passed in Congress in 1990, this federal civil rights law aims to eliminate discrimination in schools and other programs that receive federal money. It requires that schools make special accommodations for students with disabilities, though it did not mention ADHD specifically. In 1991, the U.S. Department of Education added ADHD to the list of disabilities covered by Section 504.

[These] "changes coincide with a dramatic rise in the number of children said to have ADHD. Between 1990 and 1992, the number of ADHD diagnoses jumped from approximately one million to over three million and the production of one drug,

Ritalin, increased from 2,000 kilos to over 8,000 kilos. As to whether there is a cause and effect, that is the question that remains to be explored."

Judith E. Heumann, Assistant Secretary for Special Education and Rehabilitative Services of the U.S. Department of Education, disagreed. The Individuals with Disabilities Education Act, she said, "does not encourage the use of Ritalin or any other medications." And "increasing the number of children who take behavioral drugs will not increase the size of a school district's IDEA grant." She did not address funding of Section 504 of the Vocational Rehabilitation Act, however.

Between 2000 and 2005, the number of prescriptions continued to increase—more than 600

PRESIDENT CLINTON SIGNED THE INDIVIDUALS WITH DISABILITIES EDUCATION ACT INTO LAW ON JUNE 4, 1997.

41

percent—and the gender gap narrowed. Males taking medicine for the disorder outnumbered females ten to one in 1985 but only five to one in 1995. As more and more girls are diagnosed with attention deficit disorder, both with and without hyperactivity, the difference in the number of boys and girls taking the drug is narrowing.

In recent years, newer drugs have eaten into Ritalin's market. In 2000, Ritalin and methylphenidate had a 54 percent share of the market. Now their market share is under 50 percent. Other forms of methylphenidate, amphetamine-based drugs, and nonstimulant ADHD drugs have become more and more popular.

Trends in Abuse
People who abuse Ritalin do so to get high, stay awake, study, party longer, lose weight, or to mix it with other drugs in order to enhance their effects, according to the U.S. Drug Enforcement Agency. Some take the drug orally, while others crush and snort Ritalin or dissolve the drug in water and inject the solution into a vein. Some people obtain pills through smuggling rings or from Internet pharmacies, which offer prescription drugs to customers without requiring a prescription, physician consultation, or verification. Ritalin is on the DEA's list of the ten most often stolen prescriptions. Most abusers can easily get Ritalin from their classmates, their friends, their children, and even by prescription. Teen abusers find ADHD drugs very easy to

get, almost as available as pain medicines such as Vicodin, OxyContin, and Tylox, though less available than marijuana. Ritalin abuse is most common among high school and college students, according to the National Drug Intelligence Center (NDIC). However, abuse among elementary and middle school students is not unknown.

Information regarding the frequency of abuse of Ritalin and other prescription stimulants nationwide is incomplete and sometimes contradictory, but Ritalin abuse among teens seems to be on the decline. NDIC figures show that Ritalin abuse among eighth graders dropped from 2.9 percent to 2.5 percent between 2001 and 2004 and from 4.8 percent to 3.4 percent among tenth graders. Among twelfth graders, Ritalin abuse dropped from 5.1 percent to 4.0 percent between 2001 and 2002. It stayed the same in 2003 and then jumped to 5.1 percent in 2004.

The Partnership Attitude Tracking Study (PATS) has tracked the abuse of Ritalin only since 2001, but that tracking suggests that the abuse of Ritalin is on the decline. Almost 30 percent of teens admit to having a friend who has used Ritalin without a prescription and 9 percent of teens have tried Ritalin or its chemical cousin Adderall during their lifetimes. But teens do realize that abusing Ritalin is not a good idea. Fifty-four percent of teens see Ritalin abuse as a great risk, compared with 48 percent who view Ecstasy, Vicodin, OxyContin, and Tylox, and 17 percent who view marijuana, as a great risk.

Monitoring the Future reported that 2.9 percent of young adults were abusing methylphenidate in both 2002 and 2003.

The Drug Abuse Warning Network (DAWN) reports on people who come to the emergency room for treatment. Its measure is the number of "mentions." A drug mention refers to a substance mentioned during an emergency room visit and does not imply abuse of the drug or that the drug was the cause of the visit. DAWN mentions for methylphenidate have decreased steadily from 1,860 in 1995 to 1,728 in 1998 to 1,279 in 2001.

Ritalin in High School
Steve did not feel well at all, standing on the quad among his classmates at a memorial service on September 11 at Antelope Valley High School in California. Suddenly, he fell to the ground and started shaking. Other students felt sluggish, nauseous, their hearts beating fast. Others threw up.

It was not the warm September sun that caused their problems. It was methylphenidate, Ritalin's generic twin. One fourteen-year-old classmate and at least one other student had brought the drugs to school and given them away or sold them. School authorities began tracking down other teens who had taken pills and confiscated between 150 and 800 pills that had been brought to school in sandwich baggies.

At least fourteen of the students who took the drug felt bad enough to be taken to area hospitals.

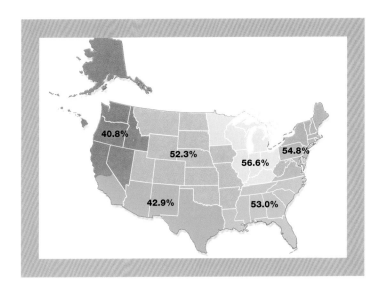

RITALIN ABUSE IN THE UNITED STATES VARIES BY REGION. SHOWN IS THE PERCENT OF REGIONAL LAW ENFORCEMENT AGENCIES THAT CONSIDER RITALIN ABUSE A PROBLEM.
SOURCE: NDTS 2004

Three ambulances, three fire engine companies, and a paramedic squad were sent to the school, where news helicopters circled overhead after word spread of the mass overdose. Before lunch, an announcement over the intercom called any teens who had taken pills to the office. They face no discipline, the announcement promised. At least three students took up the offer, officials said. Some of the students swallowed a handful of pills, while others said they had taken only a few.

Even before the students overdosed, there were pills circulating on campus, one student said. His friend swallowed a handful of methylphenidate, sleeping pills, the pain killer Vicodin, and LSD during first-period gym class and fainted, the student said. "He just passed out and his eyes were rolled up in his head. That's when I went and got Security." Three other students took methylphenidate and Vicodin at the same time, but not as much. Anyone who was found to have distributed the pills faced suspension, transfer to other schools, or expulsion. The teens who brought the pills to school faced criminal charges.

Some high school students have begun using other students' Ritalin as a study drug. They use it to concentrate, to stay up late to write papers, and to study for exams. More than 7 percent of the 1,304 Palo Alto High School students surveyed said they had used ADHD drugs without a prescription at least once.

"It's like caffeine or Red Bull," said a senior who hides the pills he gets from a friend in a tin of breath mints. "It's like any other pick-me-up."

Possessing Ritalin and other ADHD medications without a prescription is illegal. So is selling it, trading it for a tank of gas, or giving it away. The law calls that distribution—and people who distribute Ritalin can find themselves paying fines and doing jail time.

It is not easy for schools to catch students who take Ritalin illegally, since principals and teachers do not know who has a prescription and who does not. This is especially true now that there are longer-acting pills on the market. Adults usually do not hear about the problem unless someone gets sick.

Ritalin Abuse in Colleges

As high school students on Ritalin and similar ADHD drugs have graduated, the incidence of abuse has moved to the college campus. Most college students who abuse Ritalin do not use it as a party drug but as a study aid. They say it gives them the energy they need to pay attention in class, study longer and harder, tackle boring material, write term papers, and cram for exams. As many as one in five college students have used Ritalin or similar drugs without a prescription.

One pre-law student pops a Ritalin pill to study for an important exam. "I could go for hours studying when I took the Ritalin," he said. "In college there is so much pressure to succeed, and . . . people want to go out and have fun, too. Sometimes you have to turn to alternative methods to succeed." Another student admitted, "I wouldn't have made it through organic chemistry without it."

Ritalin is not difficult to find on college campuses. Students with prescriptions give the pills to friends or sell them "for five dollars a pill or something ridiculous," said one student. And student health center doctors will often prescribe the drug after a brief consultation, a "five to ten question true/false test," as one student put it.

Some students buy Ritalin because they believe they have undiagnosed ADD or ADHD. Others feel that the stress of performing at the college level justifies taking amphetamines or Ritalin. But this rationalization makes other students mad.

A College for Students with ADHD

Alex had ADHD and was a very good student. He wanted to attend a college where there was a chance of success. But what college would take him? Where could he succeed? "A year ago, I was going nowhere fast," Alex said. "I was perceived as a failure. I had given up." He discovered Landmark College in Putney, Vermont, one of the only nationally accredited institutions of higher learning, specifically designed for students who learn differently. At Landmark, Alex found that he could achieve his academic goals. There, he learned that hard work pays off and to never give up. "I was a high-risk student," he said, "and Landmark College gave me a second chance. It opened the door to the future for me."

Landmark College enrolls bright, capable, and motivated students with documented learning disabilities and ADHD. They want students who have the intelligence and ability to earn a college degree but who may not have the educational skills to match. They want students who have the dedication to succeed in school and in the workforce. "You bring the desire to learn—and we'll provide the tools for you to do so," says the college's Web site. "Landmark College teaches you how to learn while you're learning."

The first graduation ceremony at Landmark College was on May 19, 1988. Landmark has two graduation ceremonies per year, one at the end of each semester. It has enrolled some three thousand students to date.

LANDMARK COLLEGE IN PUTNEY, VERMONT, IS A COLLEGE SPECIFICALLY DESIGNED FOR STUDENTS WITH LEARNING DISABILITIES.

"Performance enhancing drugs are not acceptable in athletics," said one University of Chicago student. "They shouldn't be acceptable in academics either."

History professor David Coffey agrees. "If such drugs do provide a real competitive edge, we need to approach it as cheating, just like we are doing with performance enhancing products in sports," he says. But other people look at it differently. For Randy Cohen, who writes an ethics column in the *New York Times*, the goal in academics is to learn as much as possible. "If I could take a pill to learn French," he says, "I'd be a fool not to."

Most college students believe they can control their Ritalin use. They are careful with it and use it only as a study drug. But some use it to party, too. "It's like speed," one student said. "They snort it. I think most people take it not to go out and party but to stay awake and work even if they don't have ADD.'"

Some have experienced uncomfortable symptoms—from erratic heartbeat to panic attacks. And a few students are starting to experience dependence and addiction.

Adult Abuse

Even adults abuse Ritalin. America watched adult abuse of Ritalin on television as Lynette Scavo, a mom on the prime time soap opera *Desperate Housewives*, took Ritalin to stay up all night to make costumes. All too often, adults abuse Ritalin in real life as well. One housewife discovered the drug when she tried out her daughter's Ritalin to see what it was like. On the drug, she had more energy than she knew what to do with. To get rid of it, "I got the entire house not only picked up but clean," she told *People* magazine. "I was down on my hands and knees, moved the furniture, scrubbed the carpet." She never tried it again, but she admits being tempted from time to time.

Another mom was trying to lose the weight she gained when she had her second baby. Maria did not have a prescription, but her oldest child did. She decided to try it. She lost fifty pounds. It seemed like a miracle. She got a prescription in her own name from her child's doctor. She took more and more, hiding pills from her family. Maria spent five months in rehabilitation to overcome her addiction.

In Minnesota, a health aide admitted to stealing five hundred Ritalin pills from a school, and in Ohio, a janitor stole forty pills from the nurse's office at the school where he worked. Teachers and principals have raided the school medicine cabinet for Ritalin as well.

"Generally speaking," says Gretchen Feussner, DEA's [Drug Enforcement Agency] Ritalin expert, "the more available a drug is, the more likely it will be abused." As long as there are millions of prescriptions of Ritalin and other ADHD stimulants across the nation, abuse will continue.

3 THE DANGERS OF RITALIN USE AND ABUSE

Taking Ritalin by mouth under the supervision of a doctor is generally safe. However, abuse of Ritalin can cause problems, including drug interactions, psychological difficulties, physical side effects, and problems getting certain jobs.

Mixing Ritalin with other drugs can cause unexpected consequences. Taking Ritalin and an antidepressant together, for example, may boost the strength of the Ritalin. Taking it with over-the-counter cold medicines that contain decongestants can cause dangerously high blood pressure or irregular heart rhythms.

Psychological Difficulties

Long-term Ritalin use carries the risk of psychological difficulties. Some children taking Ritalin feel

52

stigmatized. They may come to believe they are handicapped or learn to be helpless, according to Dr. David Stein, author of *Ritalin Is Not the Answer*. Some middle-school students who have been on Ritalin since early in elementary school can come to believe that they have to have the drug to do well in school, to pay attention in class, or to function at all. On the other hand, many children feel empowered by their diagnosis and treatment. There is finally a label for what is wrong with them, and there is a solution for it as well.

One study on rats has also suggested that early use of Ritalin may make it more likely that children will suffer from depression as they grow older. The study found that early exposure to Ritalin and similar stimulant drugs seems to alter the brains of rats and cause changes in behavior that last into adulthood.

"Rats exposed to Ritalin as juveniles showed large increases in learned-helplessness behavior during adulthood, suggesting a tendency toward depression," said William A. Carlezon Jr., Ph.D., the Harvard Medical School professor who led the study. The drug may short-circuit the brain's reward system and make it difficult to experience pleasure, which is a "hallmark symptom of depression."

Another study at the University of California at Berkeley followed five hundred children for more than twenty-five years and suggests that the use of Ritalin in childhood may increase the likelihood that young people will smoke cigarettes or abuse cocaine or stimulants—as much as doubling the risk. A four-year study at Harvard disputes those findings. This study of five children between the ages of ten and fifteen suggests the opposite, that children with ADHD who do not take Ritalin are much more likely to use illegal drugs.

Side Effects
Children who take Ritalin—even legally—may suffer physical side effects. Some children experience stunted growth. Ritalin can reduce children's appetites or alter the natural balance of the body's growth hormones. Children often take summer holidays from Ritalin, just as they do from school, in order to catch up on height and weight gains. A 2004 study at the University of California at Berkeley found that over a two-year period, children who took stimulants grew more than half an inch less and gained at least eight pounds less than those who did not take the drugs. However, the American Academy of Pediatrics suggests that though Ritalin does not cause a significant reduction of height in the long run, long-term use of stimulants can result in weight loss.

Some children and teenagers experience rebound. Once they metabolize Ritalin and the level of the drug in the bloodstream goes down, children go back to being excitable and impulsive, and up to half feel agitated enough that they have trouble sleeping. Decreasing the last dose of the day can help.

Many children taking Ritalin develop tics, involuntary muscle contractions and movements of the arms and legs. These symptoms often don't go away when the Ritalin is stopped, so it may be that the tics are the result of ADHD, not the medication. There may be a possible link to liver cancer. In a 1995 study, adult mice developed liver abnormalities and tumors, including highly aggressive, rare cancers. However, no study has yet shown a link between Ritalin and cancer in humans.

Though serious side effects are very uncommon, humans taking Ritalin have experienced heart tissue damage. Ritalin can have persistent cumulative effects on the myocardium, the muscle cells that form the lining of the heart wall. Stephanie started taking Ritalin in first grade and took her medicine faithfully until the day she died of cardiac arrhythmia at age eleven. The day before, her doctor had increased her dose.

Career Issues

A history of Ritalin use can cause problems when people look for certain jobs—jobs that require a security clearance from the government and military service. Taking Ritalin torpedoed one young man's dreams. Christopher dreamed of joining the Coast Guard, but when he went to enlist, he was rejected because of his history of drug use. The drug: Ritalin. Christopher took the drug daily from the time he was about twelve years old, not because he was hyperactive, but because his parents were worried that he was not doing well enough in school. They thought it would improve his concentration. "I was shocked and disappointed," Christopher said. "I didn't expect Ritalin to affect my future like this."

When Christopher tried to join the Coast Guard, the United States was not at war. But since the war in Iraq has made it difficult for the military to recruit the soldiers it needs, some branches of the service are rethinking the issue. People who have been off the drug for a period of time may be able to get a medical waiver, but there is no guarantee.

Dangers: Abuse

On the surface, abusing Ritalin may not seem especially risky. After all, millions of kids take the drug every day. How harmful can it be? It is easy to tell the exact strength of each Ritalin pill. And Ritalin is clean—every ingredient, active and inactive, is listed in the literature packaged with the drug—unlike street drugs. It is impossible to know how strong street drugs are or what ingredients they contain.

Physical Dangers

When abused, Ritalin can be addictive. Tolerance—the need for more and more of the drug to get the same effect—develops rapidly in abusers. The physical effects of Ritalin abuse can be unpredictable. They may include agitation, inability to sleep, abdominal cramps, nausea, exhaustion, increased

Street Names

Crackers	LSD; Talwin and Ritalin combination is injected and produces an effect similar to the effect of heroin mixed with cocaine
JIF	Ritalin
Kiddie Cocaine	Ritalin
MPH	Ritalin, methylphenidate
One and Ones	Talwin and Ritalin combination is injected and produces an effect similar to the effect of heroin mixed with cocaine
Pharming	Consuming a mixture of prescription substances
Poor man's heroin	Talwin and Ritalin combination is injected and produces an effect similar to the effect of heroin mixed with cocaine
Ritz and Ts	A combination of Ritalin and Talwin injected
Set	Place where drugs are sold; Talwin and Ritalin combination is injected and produces an effect similar to the effect of heroin mixed with cocaine
Ts and Rits	Talwin and Ritalin combination is injected and produces an effect similar to the effect of heroin mixed with cocaine
Ts and Rs	Talwin and Ritalin combination is injected and produces an effect similar to the effect of heroin mixed with cocaine
Vitamin R	Ritalin (methylphenidate)
West Coast	Methylphenidate (ritalin)

THOUGH RARE, RITALIN CAN CAUSE HEART TISSUE DAMAGE. TAKEN LONG ENOUGH, RITALIN CAN DAMAGE THE MUSCLE CELLS THAT LINE THE HEART WALL.

blood pressure, tremors, increased body temperature, hallucinations, convulsions, seizures, and heartbeat irregularities.

The filler in Ritalin tablets, which is not meant to be injected, may cause lesions at the injection site, as well as breathing difficulties. In the worst cases, Ritalin abuse can cause seizures—most commonly following intravenous use, stroke, or heart attack—even the first time a person abuses the drug.

In February 2006, the issue of sudden death came to the nation's attention when an advisory panel recommended that the FDA put a "black box" warning on ADHD drugs such as Ritalin. Such drugs may have been involved in fifty-four cases of heart attack, stroke, hypertension, heart palpitation, and arrhythmia in adults and children and as many as twenty-five deaths—including the deaths of nineteen children—between 1999 and 2003. Another twenty-six deaths between 1969 and 2003 in medicated ADHD patients involved suicide, intentional overdose, drowning, heat stroke, and underlying diseases. The panel was also concerned that no studies lasted long enough or included enough patients to evaluate the long-term effects of stimulants on the heart.

These concerns, added to the fact that doctors write more than 30 million prescriptions for the drugs each year, led the panel to recommend the FDA's strongest warning—that a drug might increase the risk of death and injury. FDA officials said that they would not act on the recommenda-tions any time soon. The risk of sudden death from Ritalin-type ADHD drugs is very low—literally one in a million, according to reports to the FDA. However, the agency admits that it probably does not hear about every death or complication from the ADHD drugs.

Psychological Dangers of Ritalin Abuse
Completely apart from physical side effects is the psychological fallout. Psychological dependence can develop quickly, especially in people who are depressed. Abuse of and withdrawal from Ritalin can cause depression, as well as psychosis that looks very much like acute paranoid schizophrenia, a very serious psychiatric disease. As many as 9 percent of abusers of Ritalin and other stimulant drugs may experience psychosis, and the psychosis and maniclike reactions that abuse causes may lead to violence and suicide.

In a manic or psychotic state, abusers can expe-rience extreme anxiety and panic, which scrambles their thinking, sometimes causing them to crash into walls, run into traffic, jump out windows, or act out in other bizarre ways that can get them hurt. In 1995, a college student crushed and snorted Ritalin, then took off all his clothes and ran naked through downtown Jackson, Mississippi. By the time police got to the scene, he was dying from a head injury. This is not to say that Ritalin causes the psychotic behavior. People who suffer such extreme reactions

Psychological dependence on Ritalin can occur quickly, making it hard to function without the medication, especially in people who are prone to depression.

61

may have psychotic vulnerabilities that have gone undetected, and Ritalin may just push them over the edge.

Mixing Ritalin with Other Drugs

Ritalin can interact in unpredictable ways with alcohol and other prescription, street, or over-the-counter drugs. On the street, some addicts mix the prescription drug Talwin, a painkiller, with Ritalin. Talwin and Ritalin are sometimes called "poor man's heroin" because prescriptions cost very little. Others, on Chicago's South Side, mix Ritalin with heroin—a "speedball"—or in combination with both cocaine and heroin for a more potent effect. Street abusers inject the mix for a high similar to that of heroin mixed with cocaine.

Injecting Talwin and Ritalin can cause dizziness, nausea, vomiting, shakiness, confusion, constipation, anorexia, insomnia, and paranoia. The high is followed by a low—emotional and physical depression. High doses of Talwin and Ritalin can raise blood pressure and cause hallucinations. Very high amounts can cause coma and even death. There is also a risk of infected veins, abscesses, or superficial skin ulcers from using dirty needles. Intravenous abusers who swap needles open themselves to the risk of HIV infection.

If filler material in Talwin and Ritalin does not dissolve, it can travel to the lungs and cause breathing problems and lung disease. The body does develop a tolerance for Ritalin and abusers need more and more to get the same effect. Withdrawal symptoms can be severe and generally include agitation, inability to sleep, abdominal cramps, nausea, anxiety, severe emotional depression, and exhaustion.

A TEACHER HELPS STUDENTS IN A CLASSROOM. STUDENT-TEACHER INTERACTION CAN HELP STUDENTS FOCUS ON THEIR WORK.

4 THE ADHD/ RITALIN DEBATE

By the 1990s, there was a virtual war over the use of Ritalin. A steady stream of newspaper and magazine articles and books condemned giving Ritalin to high-spirited children in the belief that this led to a loss of natural childhood exuberance. Some—without any scientific evidence to back up their claims—maintained that Ritalin causes permanent brain damage.

With so many students taking Ritalin—two or three kids per classroom across the United States— the debate is important to a lot of people. Parents worry they are doing the wrong thing for their children. Those who deal every day with children with ADHD have formed strong opinions through their experiences. Some do not believe that ADHD exists.

So the debate can be passionate and irrational. Sometimes it is difficult to find middle ground.

The heart of the debate goes to three questions about Ritalin. Is it reasonable to have children take Ritalin? Is Ritalin safe? And is the medical establishment and drug industry responsible in recommending Ritalin?

The Medical Establishment Answer

The medical establishment says yes to all three questions. It is reasonable to have children with attention deficit disorders take Ritalin. Some six thousand studies have convinced the American Medical Association, the American Academy of Pediatrics, and the American Academy of Child and Adolescent Psychiatry that ADHD is a legitimate diagnosis and that Ritalin is an appropriate treatment.

"There is no controversy among practicing scientists," says Dr. Russell Barkley, professor of psychiatry at the State University of New York Upstate Medical University at Syracuse and author of *Taking Charge of ADHD*. "No scientific meetings mention any controversies about the disorder, about its validity as a disorder, about the usefulness of using stimulant medications like Ritalin for it. There simply is no controversy. The science speaks for itself."

Some people "say that ADHD can't be real—that it can't be a valid disorder—because there's no lab measure for it," Barkley continues. "But that's tremendously naïve. A disorder doesn't have to have a blood test to be valid. If that were the case, all mental disorders would be invalid. Schizophrenia, manic depression, and Tourette's Syndrome would all be fakes. There is no blood test or x-ray for any mental disorder right now in our science. That doesn't make them invalid." Doctors approach these diseases in the same way they do ADHD. They listen to the patients' history and their complaints, compare the symptoms with the disease, and rule out other possible explanations.

The medical and scientific communities generally believe that Ritalin is safe and effective when taken as prescribed by a doctor who has done a thorough examination and ruled out other causes for a child's ADHD symptoms. Reputable studies as well as fifty years of experience have shown Ritalin's side effects to be generally short-term. Doctors are often able to reduce side effects simply by changing the dose or schedule for taking the drug, or changing to a different medication.

There is some worry, notably on the part of the Centers for Disease Control, about the number of people taking drugs like Ritalin for years and years. There are no truly long-term controlled studies, and there may never be any, because withholding treatment from a control group of ADHD sufferers for years would not be ethical. However, Ritalin has been on the market for a long time with few reports of serious problems stemming from long-term use.

Today, ADHD is generally considered to have a strong biological base, and recent studies at Harvard

Medical School have looked at a defect in the DNA of afflicted individuals. But child psychiatrists continue to stress the need to include treatments besides Ritalin—especially individual and family counseling—in the treatment of children with ADD/ADHD. Most agree that it would be wrong to deny them access to a drug that has helped overcome the symptoms of ADHD for a very long time.

The Critics Answer
Critics disagree. Many believe it is not reasonable to prescribe Ritalin for children because they don't think that ADHD exists. Dr. Peter Breggin, one of the most outspoken critics of Ritalin, calls ADHD a fake disease. "This diagnosis [ADHD] was created for the specific purpose of suppressing children," he says. "Every single item in the list of symptoms has to do with controlling large groups of children in classroom settings. Could it be a defect in the brain that makes you do everything a teacher can't stand? We've got a disease that goes away if you act in an interesting, warm, caring, engaging way with these kids."

Critics continue to point out that there is no blood test, x-ray, or brain scan that can definitively diagnose ADHD. However, researchers using magnetic resonance imaging (MRI) may be close to finding evidence in brain scans that could reliably confirm or rule out whether someone has ADD or ADHD. Even if ADHD does exist, many critics claim, doctors do not spend the time to find out what is really wrong with the kids. After a fifteen-minute consultation or a checklist rundown, they diagnose children and prescribe powerful drugs. Many people who support prescribing Ritalin to children agree with critics on this point.

Critics say that Ritalin is too dangerous a drug to give to children. They claim that no one knows enough about how Ritalin affects the developing brains of children for prescribing it to be responsible. Studies point to evidence that Ritalin may suppress children's growth in both height and weight; however, growth suppression and weight loss are generally minor. Ritalin may also make children prone to depression later in life, one long-term study found. And no wonder, say critics. Ritalin is similar to amphetamines and cocaine in the way it acts on the body and brain.

Even when it does not cause serious medical side effects, Ritalin is a drug that steals childhoods, says Breggin, and prescribing it is the equivalent of chemically straitjacketing children. When laboratory animals are put on Ritalin, he points out, "they stop playing. They stop being curious. They stop trying to escape. We make good caged animals with these drugs, and we make good caged kids by knocking the spontaneity out of them."

Critics argue that there are better choices than Ritalin. However, some of the alternatives they recommend are actually treatments for other problems that may masquerade as ADHD. Sensory Integration Training (SIT) can help children whose brain is overloaded with too much input. Treatment for lead helps children with high levels of lead in their system. Eliminating certain foods can help children with food allergies. Thyroid treatment can help if the thyroid gland is not working properly. But these are not treatments for ADHD.

Other alternatives have no scientific studies to back them up. No research supports antimotion sickness medication, treatment for candida yeast, chiropractic adjustment, optometric vision training—training the eyes, or nutritional supplements, which may do more harm than good.

Several alternatives have shown promise in early studies, but more research is needed. Interactive Metronome Training, in which children match the beat of a metronome, helped. Boys who received IMT show improvements in a wide range of areas. Neurofeedback, in which patients learn to increase the arousal levels in specific regions of the brain, has shown promise in a number of studies, though more rigorous studies are needed to clarify that it works specifically with ADHD. Finally, if a deficiency of the polyunsaturated fatty acids Omega-3 and Omega-6 in the nerve cell membranes of the brain are to blame for ADHD, as some researchers think, then fatty acid supplements could be helpful. Further controlled studies can shed some light on this alternative treatment.

The pharmaceutical industry comes in for strong criticism. Breggin compares drug companies with the tobacco and alcohol industry. Their priority, he says, is not the children who take the drugs they sell, but their own profits. "They're selling a product," Breggin says. They "withhold information from the public and give distorted views of their drugs. They'll stand on their heads to get their drugs approved."

Nor do critics trust the medical establishment when it comes to Ritalin and similar drugs. They charge that pharmaceutical companies have bought and paid for researchers and doctors who speak well of Ritalin. And they discount scientific studies suggesting Ritalin's safety and effectiveness, suggesting that the results of such studies are fixed in advance. Dr. Breggin asserts that the multimillion dollar National Institute of Mental Health MTA study was "basically worthless," even though the researchers were independent and had no vested interest in finding positive results.

Such criticisms are worth considering, but millions have taken Ritalin and other methylphenidate drugs. Hundreds of studies have found it to be relatively safe, writes Barkley, but that does not mean Ritalin has no side effects. Even aspirin has side effects. Except in very rare cases with histories of serious cardiac problems, the side effects of taking Ritalin are mainly annoying and not life threatening. Ritalin remains "among the safest medications used in psychiatry and pediatrics, including some over-the-counter medications."

AUTHOR ELIZABETH WURTZEL, WHO BECAME FAMOUS FOR HER WRITINGS ON DEPRESSION, AT ONE TIME BECAME ADDICTED TO RITALIN. SHE WROTE ABOUT THAT AS WELL.

5 RECOVERY AND TREATMENT

Elizabeth Wurtzel was a famous author. She frequently appeared on cable news shows and late night television. But that did not keep her from becoming an abuser of Ritalin. Her drug of choice was cocaine before she discovered that she could use Ritalin as a substitute. She wrote in her book, *More, Now, Again*: "I didn't see addiction coming. The pills were safe. Even the *Physician's Desk Reference* barely mentions that Ritalin has the potential for 'psychological dependence.' I didn't see Ritalin creeping up. I thought it was a free ride." When Wurtzel realized she was hooked, she checked herself into a treatment center—several times—for long-term treatment.

Overdose and withdrawal from Ritalin can be miserable as well as causing serious medical problems. People who are unconscious from drug overdose must be taken immediately to an emergency room. Emergency personnel provide mouth-to-mouth resuscitation, oxygen, and other life-support systems on the way to the hospital if this is necessary.

People who have overdosed on Ritalin may be disoriented. They may not be able to remember what they have been doing in the past hours or weeks. They are agitated and show poor judgment. They are usually uncoordinated; their speech may be slurred. They may be shaking or unable to keep their balance. Depending on how much of the drug they have in their system, they may have trouble breathing. Their circulatory system may collapse, and they may go into a coma.

The first thing emergency room staff does is to evaluate the seriousness of the emergency. If the overdose is life-threatening, they provide immediate medical care to prevent death. For serious overdose, they hospitalize patients for treatment and further evaluation. For overdoses that are serious but do not require hospitalization, the emergency staff evaluates patients and usually refers them for outpatient treatment.

Part of the evaluation is a drug history. Medical personnel ask patients or someone who knows them what drugs they have taken. How much have they taken? Did a doctor prescribe the drugs? Do they use street drugs? Alcohol? They also take a medical history. What diseases have patients had? Do they have diabetes? Seizure disorders? Have they overdosed before? Have they participated in treatment programs? How often?

Whether or not patients have ever used intravenous drugs is important to know, since those who have used needles to abuse drugs must be screened for the AIDS virus and hepatitis C. This is important for the safety and proper treatment of the patient as well as for the safety of the health care workers and other patients. It is also important to keep these serious diseases from spreading into the community. After emergency room staff treat patients medically, they evaluate their emotional state. Was the overdose a suicide attempt? Are they suicidal? Should patients be sent to a mental health or other special facility?

Withdrawal

Withdrawal is what happens when people stop taking a drug to which they are addicted. For some patients, like Bruce, withdrawal is unpleasant. Bruce experienced withdrawal every time he stopped taking Ritalin. His main symptom: a feeling that his attention deficit returned and was worse than before he started taking medication. However, once he learned what to expect, he found it easier to deal with the withdrawal. He knew that he did not have to worry, that there was a reason for the way he was feeling and that he would eventually "level out."

For others—especially those who abuse Ritalin—withdrawal can be terrifying. These patients are disoriented, confused, and panicky. Some become psychotic and hallucinate and experience delusions. Those patients who are behaving unpredictably are treated in a hospital, where staff can administer drugs to counter the effects of withdrawal on their central nervous system.

Emergency room staff try to find a quiet place for the patient. They do not leave the patient alone in an area that could be unsafe. Throughout treatment, they try to make eye contact and talk to patients in a quiet, supportive way. Friends or counselors who are former drug users or who have experience treating people who abuse drugs can also help talk the patient down.

To decrease patients' anxiety and sense of alienation, emergency room personnel may gently hold or touch patients. They tell them where they are and what time it is, sometimes again and again, in order to bring them to reality. They tell patients to keep their eyes open and to focus on a specific object. They ask them to describe what they are experiencing. They explain what medications and injections they give.

If the patient attacks others, staff take immediate action to control the patient and protect others. If the patient is calm enough, emergency room staff first do a physical examination and take the patient's history. Throughout, the staff maintain a calm, reassuring, and soothing manner.

Treatment

Emergency medical treatment can save lives, but it does not immediately solve the problem of Ritalin abuse. To help prevent future emergencies and pos-

VARIOUS FORMS OF THERAPY AND COUNSELING CAN BE HELPFUL FOR THOSE WHO HAVE ABUSED RITALIN.

sible death, treatment is necessary to help patients recognize their addiction to Ritalin and realize how dangerous continued abuse can be. Treatment goals include improved social interaction and meaningful relationships with other people, improvement of family relationships, and healthier ways of coping with stress and the temptation to abuse drugs. They should be drug-free and ready to go back to school or work. Addiction to any drug, illicit or prescribed, is a brain disease. Successful treatment usually includes counseling to change behavior and medication to make quitting easier.

Treating addiction to Ritalin and other prescription stimulants often focuses on the same behavioral therapies that have been effective for treating addiction to cocaine or methamphetamine. Behavioral intervention teaches addicts how to function without drugs, how to handle cravings, how to avoid drugs and situations that could lead to drug use, how to avoid relapse, and how to handle a relapse if it happens. Effective behavioral treatment may include individual, family, or group counseling. It can also help those who abuse Ritalin with their personal relationships as well as their ability to function at home, at school, and at work. So far there are no proven medications for the treatment of stimulant addiction. Since patients often suffer depression in the early days of abstinence from stimulants, doctors sometimes prescribe antidepressants.

In general, programs begin with detoxification—reducing the amount of Ritalin they take little by little and treating withdrawal symptoms. Once addicts are clean, they can begin one of a number of therapies to change their long-term behavior. One kind of behavior therapy is contingency management. Contingency management lets patients earn vouchers for drug-free urine tests. They can trade the vouchers for items they want—a higher salary at work if their employer is involved or small prizes such as socks, nail polish, bus tokens, and gift certificates for fast food, for example—as long as those things promote recovery and healthy living. Cognitive-behavioral intervention focuses on modifying how patients think, what they expect, and how they behave. It also helps them increase coping skills. Many recovering addicts take advantage of support groups, which they continue after they complete treatment.

Breaking an addiction is not easy, and many addicts need more than one time in treatment before they break their addiction.

Teens Helping Teens

Teens who suspect a friend is abusing Ritalin should not pretend that a problem does not exist. They should talk to their friend and pass the information on to the friend's parents or a trusted adult. "One of the worst things you can do is bury your head in the sand," says Gretchen Feussner of the DEA.

Do You Need Help?

- Have you ever felt the need to cut down on your use of Ritalin?
- Have you ever felt annoyed by remarks your friends or loved ones made about your use of Ritalin?
- Have you ever felt guilty or remorseful about your use of Ritalin?
- Have you ever used Ritalin as a way to "get going" or to "calm down"?

Adapted from J. A. Ewing, "Detecting Alcoholism: The CAGE Questionnaire."

Signs of Ritalin abuse are similar to those of heroin or cocaine. They include:

- fatigue
- repeated health complaints
- red or glazed eyes
- personality change
- sudden mood changes
- irritability
- irresponsible behavior
- poor judgment
- depression
- general lack of interest
- starting arguments
- negative attitude
- breaking rules

- withdrawing from family
- secretiveness
- decreased interest in school
- drop in grades
- many absences
- truancy
- discipline problems
- new friends who make poor decisions and are not interested in school or family activities
- problems with the law
- changes to less conventional styles in dress and music

Teens who find a friend or classmate unconscious from Ritalin overdose should immediately take the person to an emergency room or—better yet—call 911 for an ambulance. Knowing how to perform cardiopulmonary resuscitation—the Red Cross and other organizations offer classes—can save lives, but paramedics can provide oxygen and other life support.

While teens wait with their friend or classmate for an ambulance, they should:
- ask anyone nearby to call an adult;
- keep the person in a quiet place where not much is going on;
- not leave the person in isolation or in a place that may be unsafe;
- establish eye contact, and use a calm, gentle attitude and voice;

- remind the person that the drug caused the bad experience and it will wear off;
- repeat and reassure again and again and again;
- remind the person where they are, what time it is and what has happened;
- talk about now, not the past or future;
- tell the person to keep eyes open and focus on a specific object;
- keep friends and other people who are experienced with drugs around to help;
- gently hold or touch the person unless they react uncomfortably to this contact;
- encourage the person to talk about what they are sensing and experiencing right now.

Long-Term Help

Over the long term, it is important for teens to educate their parents. Parents can provide support later if teens are tempted to experiment or if friends are abusing Ritalin. They should keep the lines of communication open with the adults in their lives. If Ritalin abuse is a problem at school, they should let a trusted adult know—discreetly.

Teens should protect their friends. The medicine cabinet is the logical place in the home for people to look for drugs. Teens can ask their parents to store drugs with a potential for abuse somewhere else. Teens who take Ritalin should not tell people who do not need to know. They should not share. They should not sell. They should not keep their medication in a place where friends or their brothers and sisters' friends might steal it. Teens who have to store their Ritalin at school should know how many pills they have and make sure all the pills are returned to them at the end of the school year.

6 THE LEGAL PICTURE

The debate over Ritalin as well as the in-creased number of people abusing the drug has led to new laws in recent years. But many of these laws are not the typical "War on Drugs" laws, which were passed more than thirty years ago. The new laws protect consumers from foreign and possibly counterfeit drugs. They also protect parents from school officials who try to force their children to take Ritalin.

The War on Drugs
The Controlled Substances Act of 1970 established a single system of control for narcotic and psychotropic drugs for the first time in the history of the United States. It also established five classifica-

tions of drugs, according to how dangerous they are, how likely they are to be abused, how likely people are to become addicted to them, and whether they had any legitimate medical use.

Ritalin and similar ADHD drugs are Schedule II drugs because they are dangerous and have the highest potential for abuse and addiction. However, they are also medically useful, so they were not considered Schedule I drugs such as heroin, ecstasy, and marijuana. In the 1960s, diverting prescription drugs to illegal use was already a problem. Many drug manufacturers produced large amounts of pharmaceuticals, which ended up in the hands of drug abusers. By 1971, the government was addressing this problem, and placing controls on how much product drug companies could make each year. In 1998, Congress passed an amendment to the Higher Education Act that denies loans, grants, and work-study jobs to students with drug convictions.

Today, the DEA maintains strict controls on the manufacture, distribution, and prescription of Ritalin. Drug companies and pharmacies must have a special license to manufacture and sell Ritalin and they must keep careful records. Physicians must keep careful records as well, and prescription refills are not allowed without a new prescription filled out by a doctor. In 1995, Ciba Geigy, the drug company now known as Novartis, asked the DEA to reclassify Ritalin from a Schedule II to a Schedule III drug. The DEA and Congress refused. Ritalin remains a Schedule II drug. Schedule III drugs have

Importing Trouble

It looked like easy money to a California family. The father slipped across the border into Mexico and carried back cheap, unregulated prescription drugs. He brought them back to his motor home in San Diego and packaged the prescriptions for shipping. He dropped them off at FedEx for delivery to the customers who had discovered the family's illegal mail-order drug business online.

But in 1998, his business hit a snag. As he, his wife, and his daughter packaged his most recent stash, agents from the FDA's Office of Criminal Investigations, U.S. Customs, and the Postal Service knocked at his door. Ritalin was just one of the drugs they found in the family motor home. They warned the family that their activities were illegal and seized the motor home but did not charge them. Instead, they monitored their activities for several more years.

Agents watched as father, mother, and daughter picked up orders and payments at a post office box, cashed money orders, and called or faxed suppliers in Tijuana, Mexico, to fill the orders. Family members continued to go to Mexico, usually smuggling the drugs back into the United States at the Tijuana/SanYsidro, California, border, the world's busiest port of entry. Sometimes they varied their routes, and alternated cars and license plates to keep from being searched.

So what was wrong with what this family did? The Federal Food, Drug, and Cosmetic Act does not allow the importation of unapproved foreign versions of drugs even when they have been approved for use in the United States. It is also against the law to bring "misbranded" drugs into the country. Misbranding means that drugs are labeled in a foreign language and do not include adequate directions for use. Finally, it is illegal to sell drugs without an appropriate doctor's prescription.

Federal agents arrested Bevins and his wife at one of their homes in Texas in 2001, and their daughter in California the next day. They seized the home and charged the three with fourteen counts of smuggling, conspiracy to import and distribute controlled substances, and introduction of misbranded drugs into the United States.

The father pleaded guilty to conspiracy to introduce misbranded drugs into interstate commerce. He was sentenced to twenty-four months in prison and three years of supervised release. The mother and daughter pleaded guilty to aiding and abetting the introduction of misbranded drugs into interstate commerce. The mother died before sentencing. The daughter was fined $500 and sentenced to three years' supervised release.

THIS DISCOUNT PHARMACY IN TIJUANA, MEXICO, IS ONE OF MANY THAT CATERS TO CUSTOMERS FROM THE UNITED STATES SHOPPING FOR LOWER-PRICED PRESCRIPTIONS.

less potential for abuse than Schedule I and II drugs. They have a currently accepted medical use in treatment in the United States. When abused, Schedule III drugs are less likely than Schedule I and II drugs to lead to physical and psychological dependence. And they do not carry the same restrictions on prescription refill.

Some people have turned to the Internet to buy Ritalin, but this is illegal. Federal law states that for prescriptions to be valid, a true doctor-patient relationship must exist and should usually involve a physical examination. Completing a questionnaire that is then reviewed by a doctor hired by an Internet pharmacy is not a legal doctor-patient relationship. Since Ritalin is a controlled substance, anyone not registered with the DEA importing the drug into the United States from a foreign country is committing a felony.

In March 2003, Representative Max Burns (R-Georgia) introduced a bill in Congress that would prohibit schools from requiring students to take Schedule II drugs as a condition of attending school. The House of Representatives passed the bill by an overwhelming margin in May 2003, but it did not pass the Senate.

In 2003, 2004, and 2005, the House of Representatives introduced the National All Schedules Prescription Electronic Reporting Act. This law would create a national electronic prescription monitoring system to track Schedule II, III, and IV drug prescriptions. Pharmacists would report information on each patient to a central administrator, along with the drug, the date, and amount; the prescribing physician; and the dispensing pharmacy. This information could help doctors to monitor patient drug use and law enforcement to investigate drug diversion. It could also track patient drug use, prescribing patterns of doctors, prescription rates, and prescription patterns for specific drugs in certain geographic locations.

The story of Paul, which his mother details in her book *Altered States: Experimental Drugs, Expendable Children*, is the kind of nightmare that led to a number of states passing laws that prevent schools from forcing children to take Ritalin. Paul, an exuberant five-year-old, entered kindergarten in 1993. Within weeks his teacher called his parents to complain that he had trouble staying on task and sitting still in his seat. She had put him in time-out again and again for talking too much.

It wasn't that Paul was bad, the teacher explained. His brain was just probably "wired in such a way" that he could not settle down and focus. He probably had a brain disorder, which, she said, was not uncommon. In fact, she told Paul's mom, nearly 30 percent of children—mostly boys—have ADD or ADHD. But there was medication that could control his behavior. The teacher suggested Paul's parents take him to a doctor who often treated children like Paul.

Paul's parents did not like the idea of putting their son on medication. They saw nothing in his behavior at home that convinced them that anything was wrong with him. They decided to work with Paul and to be stricter with him at home before they followed his teacher's suggestion. Their decision did not sit well with the school, however, and a few weeks later the principal called. The school would suspend Paul if his behavior did not improve. His teacher insisted that they take Paul to a doctor or face charges of medical neglect.

Paul's parents made an appointment with the doctor his teachers had recommended. "When we arrived at [the doctor's] office, there was a video playing about children with ADD, explaining what teachers look for and how the disorder is more evident at school than at home," his mother wrote in her diary.

Paul was fidgety at the doctor's office, and the doctor prescribed Ritalin. His mother was not happy, but, his doctor explained, "A hyperactive child cannot sit still long enough to learn and is very disruptive to the rest of the class." Paul's mother agreed to give her son the pills.

Paul's parents were not the only ones forced to put their children on Ritalin during the 1980s and the 1990s or charged with neglect if they did not. Slowly a backlash grew, until hundreds of parents went to court, complained to their legislators, and wrote letters to their school boards demanding the right to decide for themselves if their children should take drugs.

By the late 1990s, though, some state governments began to challenge schools' authority. In 1999, the Colorado State Board of Education passed a resolution urging schools not to pressure parents to put their children on drugs but rather to focus instead on effective classroom discipline. The resolution had no legal effect, but it was the first time a government body officially stated its concern about how much Ritalin and other drugs schoolchildren take.

In 2001, Minnesota became the first state to pass laws forbidding teachers and other school staff from recommending drugs for individual students. School employees can still suggest that parents take their child to a doctor, but they may not recommend Ritalin or other specific drugs. Connecticut, North Carolina, Utah, and the Hawaii legislature passed similar legislation later the same year.

Illinois and Virginia passed similar laws in 2002. The Illinois law also prohibits school boards from taking disciplinary action against parents who refuse to give their children Ritalin or other psychotropic drugs.

Fifteen states introduced twenty-four bills and/or resolutions in 2003, including Alaska, California, Colorado, Hawaii, Indiana, Kentucky, Massachusetts, Michigan, New Hampshire, New York, North Carolina, Oregon, Texas, Vermont, and West Virginia.

In 2003, Texas, Oregon, and Colorado passed similar laws prohibiting school personnel from recommending drugs such as Ritalin or suggesting a particular diagnosis. In Texas, schools cannot keep students out of class because their parents refuse to allow them to have a psychiatric evaluation or refuse to let them take drugs. The law does not bar school health professionals from recommending that children be evaluated.

Class Action Lawsuits

In 2000, New Jersey families sued Novartis, the company that manufactures Ritalin; the American Psychiatric Association; and Children and Adults with attention deficit disorder (CHADD) for conspiring to overdiagnose ADD in order to increase Ritalin sales. They claimed that Novartis had pushed the psychiatric association to define ADHD as an illness, so that the company could profit by selling a treatment for it. They also claimed that Novartis gave hundreds of thousands of dollars to CHADD. They called CHADD a "front" for Novartis, and said the group's aim was to convince parents to medicate their children with Ritalin and similar drugs. Families filed similar class-action suits in California and Texas. Judges dismissed all of the cases as nuisance lawsuits.

Judges had dismissed the nuisance lawsuits against Novartis by 2005, but the interest in using legislatures and the courts to deal with the question of who takes Ritalin did not subside.

A Final Word

There is no doubt that many consider Ritalin a useful drug. There is no doubt that some parents and teachers see it as a quick-fix for children who cause trouble at home and at school. However, Ritalin is generally safe and children with ADHD will continue to benefit from it. Researchers will continue to study its effects on the body and the brain, and critics will continue to speak out about its use.

As with any drug, Ritalin works differently on different people, and it is up to doctors and parents—and young people themselves—to learn as much as they can about the drug and to watch carefully for negative side effects. It is critical to make sure that doctors screen for heart issues before prescribing Ritalin. It is also important for teens to take all prescriptions responsibly and to avoid joining the growing number of young people abusing Ritalin and other prescription drugs.

GLOSSARY

adrenalin—A hormone secreted (made) by the adrenal gland. It makes the heart beat faster and can raise blood pressure.

amphetamine—A colorless, volatile liquid, $C_9H_{13}N$, used as a central nervous system stimulant.

attention deficit disorder (ADD)—A syndrome, usually diagnosed in childhood, characterized by a persistent pattern of impulsiveness, a short attention span, and often hyperactivity, which interferes with academic, occupational, and social performance.

attention deficit hyperactivity disorder (ADHD)—Attention deficit disorder in which hyperactivity is present.

dopamine–A neurotransmitter formed in the brain and essential to the normal functioning of the central nervous system.

drug court–A special court responsible for handling (usually) non-violent crimes committed by people who are dependent on illegal drugs.

methylphenidate–A drug, $C_{14}H_{19}NO_2$, chemically related to amphetamine, which works to stimulate the central nervous system.

neurotransmitter–A chemical substance, such as acetylcholine or dopamine, which transmits nerve impulses across a synapse.

paranoid psychosis–A severe mental disorder, similar to schizophrenia, which is characterized by derangement of personality, loss of contact with reality, and an unfounded or exaggerated distrust of others.

stimulant–A drug or chemical that temporarily arouses or accelerates physiological or organic activity.

synapse–The junction across which nerve impulses pass from an axon terminal to a neuron.

tolerance–An adaptation in which exposure to a drug causes changes that result in a reduction in one or more of a drug's effects over time.

FURTHER INFORMATION

Books

Beal, Eileen. *Everything You Need to Know About ADD/ADHD*. New York: Rosen Publishing Group, 1998.

——. *Ritalin: Its Use and Abuse*. New York: Rosen Publishing Group, 2002.

Colleges with Programs for Students with Learning Disabilities or Attention Deficit Disorders. Lawrenceville, NJ: Peterson's, 2003.

Dendy, Chris A. Zeigler. *A Bird's-Eye View of Life with ADD and ADHD: Advice from Young Survivors!: A Reference Book for Children and Teenagers*. Cedar Bluff, AL: Cherish the Children, 2003.

Kravets, Marybeth. *The K & W Guide to Colleges for Students with Learning Disabilities and ADD*. New York: Random House, Inc., 2003.

Mooney, Jonathan and David Cole. *Learning Outside the Lines: Two Ivy League Students with Learning Disabilities and ADHD Give You the Tools for Academic Success and Educational Revolution*. New York: Simon & Schuster, 2000.

Pigache, Philippa. *ADHD*. Heinemann Library, 2004.

Quinn, Patricia O. *Putting on the Brakes: Young People's Guide to Understanding Attention Deficit Hyperactivity Disorder (ADHD)*. New York: Magination Press, 2001.

Web Sites
Children and Adults with Attention-Deficit/ Hyperactivity Disorder (CHADD)
Federation of Families for Children's Mental Health
8181 Professional Place, Suite 150
Landover, MD 20785
(800) 233-4050
http://www.chadd.org

National Information Center for Children and Youth with Disabilities (NICHCY)
P.O. Box 1492
Washington, DC 20013
(800) 695-0285
http://www.nichcy.org

ADHD Resources
ADD Warehouse
(800) 233-9273
http://www.addwarehouse.com

Children and Adults with Attention Deficit Disorders
499 N.W. 70th Ave., Suite 101, Plantation, FL 33317
(800) 233-4050
http://www.chadd.org

National Attention Deficit Disorder Association
(847) 432-2332
http://www.add.org

National Institute of Mental Health
Room 7C-02, 5600 Fishers Lane,
Rockville, MD 20857
(301) 443-4513
http://www.nimh.nih.gov

BIBLIOGRAPHY

"A Parent's Nightmare: Losing a Child to Drug-Induced Psychosis," *Education Reporter*, June 2002, No. 197, http://www.eagleforum.org/educate/2002/june02/drug-induced.shtml

Adams, Jim. "Health aide charged with stealing Ritalin," *Star Tribune* (Twin Cities), February 8, 2001.

American Academy of Pediatrics. "Clinical Practice Guideline: Diagnosis and Evaluation of the Child With Attention-Deficit/Hyperactivity Disorder," *Pediatrics*, May 2000.

American Psychiatric Association. *Diagnostic and Statistical Manual of Mental Disorders*, 4th ed., Arlington, VA: American Psychiatric Publishing, 2000.

Barkley, Russell A. "A Review of Stimulant Drug Research with Hyperactive Children," *Journal of Child Psychology and Psychiatry*, February 1977.

——. *Taking Charge of ADHD*, New York: Guilford Press, 2000.

Beal, Eileen. *Everything You Need to Know About ADD/ADHD*, New York: Rosen Publishing Group, 1998.

——. *Ritalin: Its Use and Abuse*, New York: Rosen Publishing Group, 2002.

Bell, D. S. "The Experimental Reproduction of Amphetamine Psychosis," *Archives of General Psychiatry*, vol. 29, pp. 35–50, July 1973.

Botonis, Greg. "Teens Overdose at School," Los Angeles *Daily News*, September 12, 2002, p. AV1.

Breggin, Peter. *Talking Back to Ritalin*, Cambridge, MA: Perseus Publishing, 2001.

Bren, Linda. "The Mexican Connection," *FDA Consumer*, April 1, 2002, U.S. Food and Drug Administration, http://www.fda.gov/fdac/departs/2002/202_irs.html.

Cherland, E., and R. Fitzpatrick. "Psychotic Side Effects of Psychostimulants: A Five-Year Review," *Canadian Journal of Psychiatry*, October 1999. Vol. 44, Issue 8, pp. 811–813.

Dendy, Chris A. Zeigler. *A Bird's-Eye View of Life with ADD and ADHD: Advice from Young Survivors!: A*

Reference Book for Children and Teenagers, Cedar Bluff, AL: Cherish the Children, 2003.

Drug Policy Information Clearinghouse. "Street Terms: Drugs and the Drug Trade," Washington, DC: Office of National Drug Control Policy, 2004.

Eaton, Sabrina, and Elizabeth Marchak. "Ritalin prescribed unevenly in U.S.," the (Cleveland) *Plain Dealer*, May 6, 2001, p. 1A.

Farley, Dixie. "Attention Disorder: Overcoming the Deficit Abuse of Attention Deficit Drug Can Be Deadly," *FDA Consumer*, July–August 1997, U.S. Food and Drug Administration, http://www.fda.gov/fdac/features/1997/597_adhd.html.

Hallowell, Edward M., and John J. Ratey. *Delivered from Distraction: Getting the Most out of Life with Attention Deficit Disorder*, New York: Ballantine Books, 2005.

Henderson, T. A., and V. W. Fischer. "Effects of Methylphenidate (Ritalin) on Mammalian Myocardial Ultrastructure," *American Journal of Cardiovascular Pathology*, January 1995.

Johnston, L. D., P. M. O'Malley, J. G. Bachman, and J. E Schulenberg. *Monitoring the Future: National Survey Results on Drug Use, 1975–2003,Volume I, Secondary School Students* (NIH Publication No. 04-5507), Bethesda, MD: National Institute on Drug Abuse, 2003.

Kravets, Marybeth. *The K & W Guide to Colleges for Students with Learning Disabilities and Attention Deficit Disorder*, New York: Random House, Inc., 2003.

Layton, Mary Jo, and Lindy Washburn. "Hyperactive' Kids: Victims of a Plot?—Lawsuit Alleges Scheme to Sell Ritalin," *The Record* (New Jersey), Oct. 1, 2000, p. A–1.

Lipkin, P. H. "Tics and Dyskinesias Associated with Stimulant Treatment in Attention-Deficit Hyper-activity Disorder," *Archives of Pediatric and Adolescent Medicine*, August 1994.

Lloyd, Jillian. "Behavior Control: State Urges Less Use of Drugs in Schools," *Christian Science Monitor*, November 19, 1999.

Lombardo, Marguerite R. "Through the Correct Lens: Understanding Overprescription of Stimulant Drugs, Their Abuse, and Where the Remedies Lie," Legal Electronic Document Archive, April 2004, http://leda.law.harvard.edu/leda/data/674/Lombardo.html

Massello, William, and Dale Carpenter. "A Fatality Due to the Intranasal Abuse of Methylphenidate (Ritalin)," *Journal of Forensic Science*, January 1999. 44(1), 220–221 (1999).

McLaughlin, Sheila. "Man Indicted in Ritalin Theft," *The Cincinnati Enquirer*, April 16, 2002, http://www.enquirer.com/editions/2002/04/16/loc_man_indicted_in.html

Meyerhoff, Michael K. "Ritalin Drug Holidays," *Journal of Child and Adolescent Psychopharmacology,* Summer 2004.

Miller, Toby, and Marie Claire Leger. "A Very Childish Moral Panic: Ritalin," *Journal of Medical Humanities,* Summer 2003. Vol. 24, Nos. 1/2, Summer 2003.

Mooney, Jonathan, and David Cole, *Learning Outside the Lines: Two Ivy League Students with Learning Disabilities and ADHD Give You the Tools for Academic Success and Educational Revolution,* New York: Simon & Schuster, 2000.

National Drug Threat Survey 2003 Report. Johnstown, PA: National Drug Intelligence Center, April 2004.

National Forensic Laboratory Information System, Drug Enforcement Administration, Office of Diversion Control, "Midyear Report 2004," Washington, DC: U.S. Department of Justice, 2004.

National Institute of Mental Health. *A Look at Attention Deficit Hyperactivity Disorder (ADHD).* NIH Publication No. 04–5429, Washington, DC: Department of Health and Human Services 2004.

National Institute of Mental Health, "Attention Deficit Hyperactivity Disorder," http://www.nimh.nih.gov/ healthinformation/adhdmenu.cfm, August 2005.

NIDA InfoFacts. "Methylphenidate (Ritalin)." National Institute on Drug Abuse, National

Institutes of Health, Washington, DC: U.S. Department of Health and Human Services, http:// www.nida.nih.gov/Infofacts/Ritalin.html 2004.

Partnership for a Drug-Free America. *Partnership Attitude Tracking Study*, Teens 2004, April 21, 2005, www.rwjf.org/research/researchdetail.jsp?id=1860

"Pharmaceuticals," National Drug Threat Assessment 2005. Johnstown, PA: National Drug Intelligence Center, February 2005, http:// www.usdoj.gov/ndic/pubs11/12620/pharma.htm

Pigache, Philippa. *ADHD*. Chicago: Heinemann Library, 2004.

Prescription Drugs: Abuse and Addiction. National Institute on Drug Abuse, National Institutes of Health, Bethesda, MD: U.S. Department of Health and Human Services, 2001, revised 2005.

Przybys, John. "DRUGS: Prescription for Trouble," *Las Vegas Review-Journal* (NV), March 9, 2001.

"Psychiatric Emergencies & Nursing Action," Part 4, National Center of Continuing Education, Inc., http://www.nursece.com/onlinecourses/9225P4.html

Quinn, Patricia O. *Putting on the Brakes: Young People's Guide to Understanding Attention Deficit Hyperactivity Disorder (ADHD)*, New York: Magination Press, 2000.

"Ritalin," Center for Substance Research, University of Maryland, www.cesar.umd.edu/cesar/drugs/ritalin.asp

Shaya, James, James Windell, and Holly Shreve Gilbert. *What You Need to Know About Ritalin*, New York: Bantam, 1999.

Silver, Larry B. *Advice to Parents on Attention-Deficit Hyperactivity Disorder*, Washington, DC: American Psychiatric Press, 1993, p. 189.

Smith, Kyle. "Don't Try This at Home: TV's *Desperate Housewives* Highlights a Troubling Trend: Moms Taking Their Kids' ADHD Pills," *People Weekly*, December 20, 2004, p. 87.

Spencer, T. J., and J Biederman. "Pharmacotherapy of Attention-Deficit Hyperactivity Disorder across the Life Cycle," Journal of the American Academy of Child and Adolescent Psychiatry, April 1996.

"Statistical Prevalence," About ADHD, National Resource Center on ADHD, undated, http://www.help4adhd.org/en/about/statistics

Still, George F. "Some Abnormal Physical Conditions in Children," *Lancet*, 1:1008–1168, 1902.

Struzzi, Diane. "Teens Learn Dangers of Ritalin Use; 10-Year-Old Dies after Snorting Stimulant at Party," *Roanoke (VA) Times*, April 24, 1995, p. C1.

Szuflita, Nick. "Ritalin Abuse Is Increasing," *Johns Hopkins Newsletter*, November 22, 2002, http://www.jhunewsletter.com

Taylor, John F. *Helping Your Hyperactive/Attention Deficit Child*. Prima Publishing, Rocklin, CA: 1994, p. 87.

Thomas, Karen. "'Let's Talk about What I Can Do': How 2 Young Grads Brought Learning Disabilities to Heel," *USA Today*, August 15, 2000.

Voreacos, David, and Mary Jo Layton, "Two Suits Target Maker of Ritalin—Allege Plot to Boost Sales," *The Record* (New Jersey), Sept. 15, 2000, p. A–1.

Wolf, Saleet. "Adderall Pervades University," November 3, 2003, *Chicago Maroon* Online Edition, http://maroon.uchicago.edu/news/articles/2003/11/03/adderall_pervades_un.php

Work, Henry H. "George Lathrop Bradley and the War over Ritalin," *Cosmos Journal*, September 11, 2001, http://www.cosmos-club.org/journals/2001/work.html

INDEX

ABOUT THE AUTHOR

Francha Roffé Menhard was a teacher for more than twenty-five years in both the United States and Japan. She has written advertisements, books, and newspaper columns. *The Facts About Ritalin* is the third book she has written for Marshall Cavendish's Drugs series. *The Facts About Inhalants* was named an Outstanding Science Book of the Year by the National Science Teachers Association. Menhard lives with her family in the shadow of the Rocky Mountains, when she is not traveling all over the world.